THIS OR THAT? History Edition

Sailing on the MAYFLOWER
A This or That Debate

by **Jessica Rusick**

CAPSTONE PRESS
a capstone imprint

Capstone Captivate is published by Capstone Press, an imprint of Capstone.
1710 Roe Crest Drive
North Mankato, Minnesota 56003
www.capstonepub.com

Library of Congress Cataloging-in-Publication Data is available on the Library of Congress website.
ISBN: 978-1-4966-8388-5 (library binding)
ISBN: 978-1-4966-8786-9 (paperback)
ISBN: 978-1-4966-8439-4 (eBook PDF)

Summary: More than 100 people left England aboard the *Mayflower* in 1620, hoping to start a new life in America. Test your decision-making skills with this or that questions about their journey!

Image Credits
Alamy: incamerastock, 25; Flickr: Boston Public Library, 6, Margalit Francus, 8, 18, Rob Bixby, 9, Virginia State Parks, 29; iStockphoto: ilbusca, 21, JoeRosh, 11; Library of Congress: Jan Jansson, Cover (background map), Library of Congress, 24; Shutterstock Images: Andreas Juergensmeier, Cover (Mayflower II), Bruno Lassus, 12, Charlotte Evelyn, 30, dude_lea, 10, Joseph Sohm, 27, JRJfin, 15, kruan, 16, Madele, 13, Michael Rosskothen, 3, Michael Sean O'Lear, Cover (Cape Cod), Morphart Creation, 14, Natalia Mylova, 17, Pantakan Sakda, 22, Primeiya, 23, smereka, 28, Stocksnapper, Cover (trunk), Tom Oliveira, 19, Triff, Cover (compass), Zoran Milic, 5 (map); Wikimedia Commons: Evans, Adelaide Bee, 26, Library of Congress, 7, Musphot, 20, Pub. by Smith's Inc., Plymouth, Mass. Tichnor Bros. Inc., Boston, Mass., 5

Design elements: Jan Jansson/Library of Congress (background map)

Editorial Credits
Editor: Rebecca Felix; Designers: Aruna Rangarajan & Tamara JM Peterson; Production Specialist: Tori Abraham

All internet sites appearing in back matter were available and accurate when this book was sent to press.

Printed in the United States of America.
PA117

A LONG, WEARY SEA VOYAGE

In September 1620, a ship called the *Mayflower* left England. It carried 102 passengers and about 30 crew members journeying to America, the New World.

But the *Mayflower* was built to carry cargo, not passengers. Passengers stayed mostly below deck while the crew sailed. It was dark and cramped. Storms made the ship **pitch** and roll.

The trip took 66 days. Passengers and crew spent the first winter living aboard the *Mayflower*. Some sailed to land every so often to explore. In spring, the crew returned to England. Those who remained founded Plymouth Colony in what is now Massachusetts.

HOW TO USE THIS BOOK

What if you had been a passenger on the *Mayflower*? What choices would you have made along the way? Do you think you would have survived?

THE MAYFLOWER LANDING

present-day
Massachusetts

KEY

Location 📍

N
W ⊕ E
S

This book is full of questions that relate to the *Mayflower*'s journey. Some of them are questions real people had to face. The questions are followed by details to help you come to a decision.

Pick one choice or the other. There are no wrong answers! But just like the passengers had to, you should think carefully about your decisions.

Are you ready? Turn the page to pick this or that!

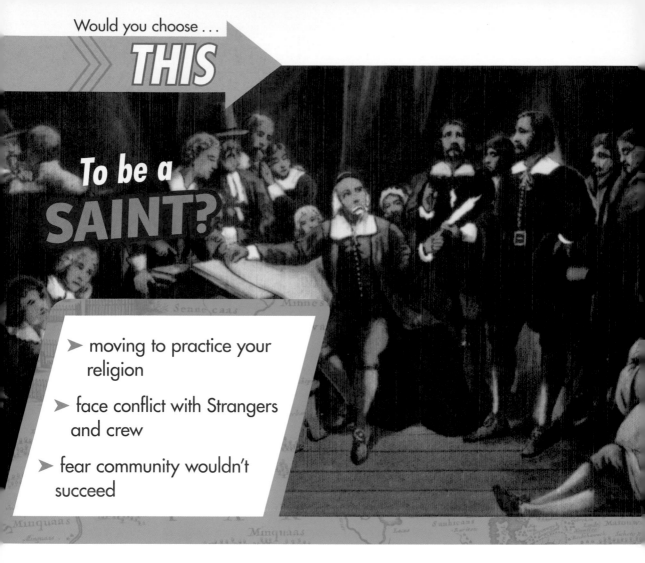

> moving to practice your religion

> face conflict with Strangers and crew

> fear community wouldn't succeed

About one-third of the people on the ship were called Saints. They traveled to America to freely practice their religion. It was dangerous for them to worship in England. There, their beliefs went against the established religion. The Saints traveled with people they called "Strangers," who didn't share the Saints' beliefs. The Saints worried these Strangers would ruin their new community.

To be a
STRANGER?

➤ seeking better ways to make money

➤ not trusted by Saints

➤ must deal with the Saints' judgmental attitude about religion

The Strangers traveled to America seeking new ways to earn a living. The Saints had judgmental attitudes toward those who did not share their religious beliefs. The Strangers would have been judged by the Saints. This attitude created **tension** aboard the ship. In North America, the Saints and Strangers had to learn to work together to survive.

Would you choose . . .

THIS

To live in
PASSENGER QUARTERS?

➤ low ceilings

➤ dark and cold

➤ people crammed together

Passengers stayed below deck on the *Mayflower*. The ceilings were only a little over 5 feet (1.6 meters) high! There were also no windows, so the space was stuffy and dark. And, with 102 people crowded together, there was little privacy in these quarters. Families were separated by curtains.

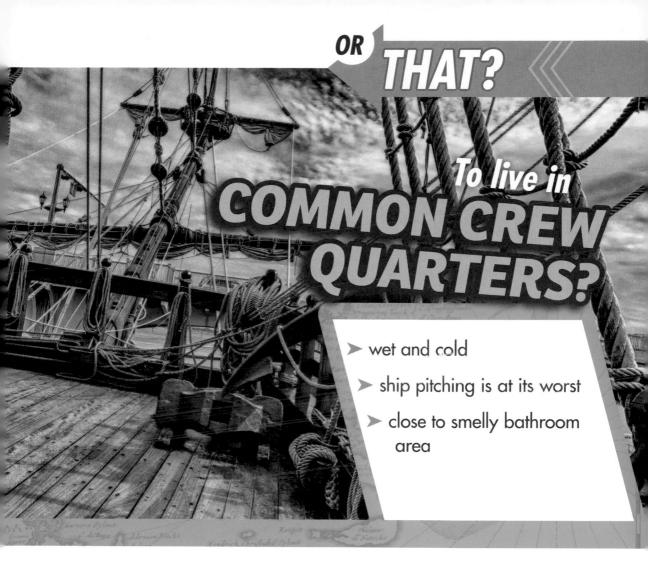

To live in
COMMON CREW QUARTERS?

> wet and cold

> ship pitching is at its worst

> close to smelly bathroom area

Some historians believe the common crew quarters were on the upper deck near the bow. The bow was constantly hit by waves, making it wet and cold there. This was also where the ship pitched the most. Pitching could make it hard for people to keep their balance. Crew quarters were also close to where the crew went to the bathroom, which was likely dirty and smelly.

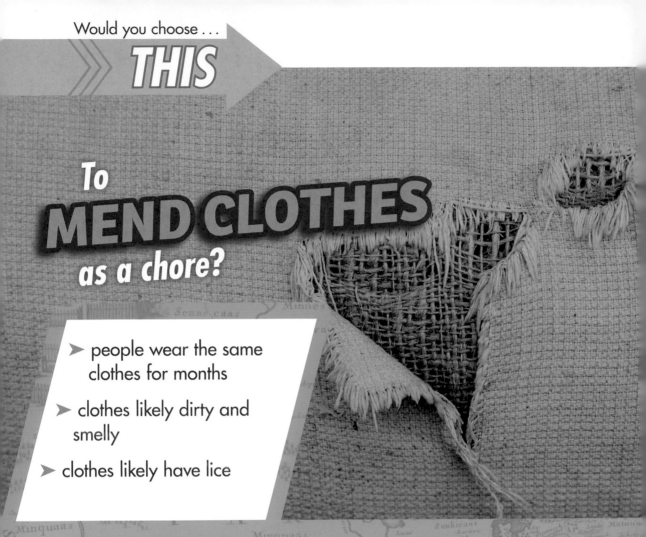

THIS

To MEND CLOTHES as a chore?

- ➤ people wear the same clothes for months
- ➤ clothes likely dirty and smelly
- ➤ clothes likely have lice

Passengers wore the same clothes for the entire journey. It was important to mend rips and tears so the clothes lasted. The clothes grew smelly. If they became wet with salt water, they became stiff. They would likely also hold body lice. These tiny bugs can live in body hair and cloth. They make people itch. Body lice could easily spread to people mending clothes.

EMPTY SLOP BUCKETS

To as a chore?

> slop buckets hold pee, poop, and vomit

> must journey above deck to empty

> possibility of spilling the smelly contents

There were no toilets on the *Mayflower*. Passengers peed, pooped, and **vomited** into slop buckets. These buckets had to be emptied regularly. Otherwise, they would overflow. Passengers went above deck to empty slop buckets into the ocean. If they weren't careful, the buckets could spill!

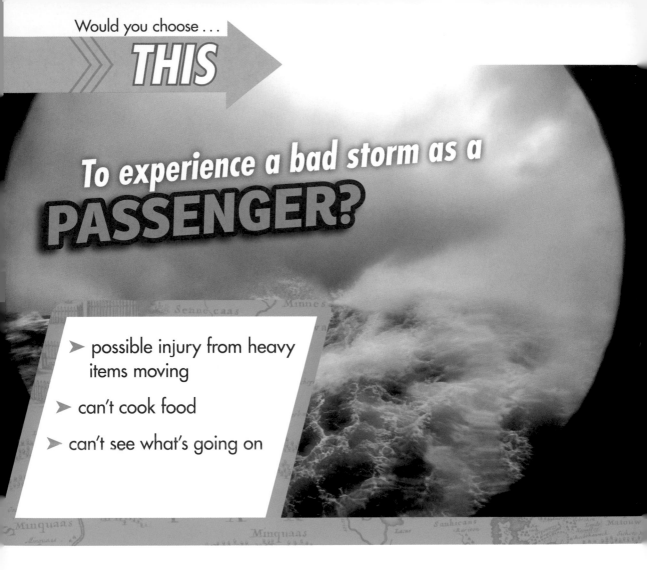

To experience a bad storm as a PASSENGER?

- ➤ possible injury from heavy items moving
- ➤ can't cook food
- ➤ can't see what's going on

Passengers stayed below deck during storms. They risked injury from heavy items on board moving due to rough waves. Since there were no windows below deck, passengers couldn't see what was going on. On calm days, passengers cooked meals over a fire in an iron box. But during a storm, this was too dangerous. Passengers ate cold food instead.

To experience a bad storm as a
CREW MEMBER?

➤ on upper decks in rain and waves

➤ must make repairs to ship

➤ risk of injury or being swept overboard

Crew members were above deck during storms. They had to sail the ship and make repairs in the rain and waves. This could include fixing sails or plugging holes. If the repairs weren't made quickly, the ship could sink or be forced to turn around. Crew members were also at risk of being swept overboard into the freezing ocean.

To suffer from

SEASICKNESS ON THE JOURNEY?

- ➤ nausea and vomiting
- ➤ wouldn't want to eat
- ➤ often can't stand up

Storms made the *Mayflower* pitch violently. Many passengers suffered from seasickness on the journey. Below deck, there was nothing passengers could do but wait for the ocean to calm. Many threw up in slop buckets and felt too sick to eat. Others were too dizzy to even stand up.

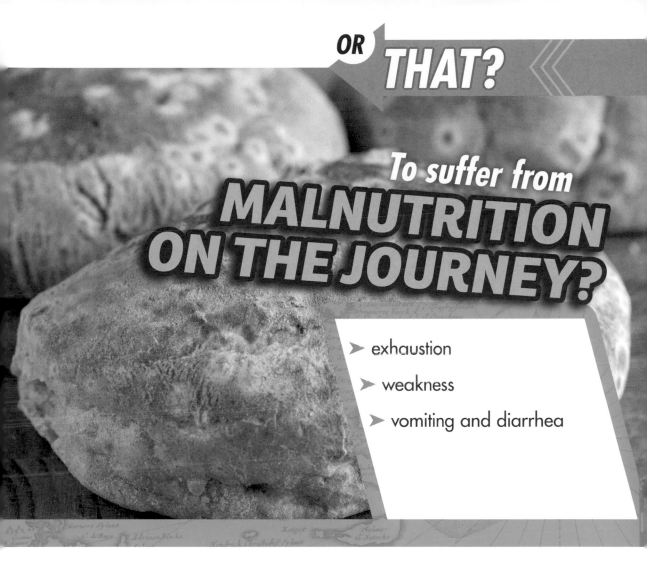

To suffer from

MALNUTRITION ON THE JOURNEY?

➤ exhaustion

➤ weakness

➤ vomiting and diarrhea

Toward the end of the journey, the *Mayflower* ran out of unspoiled dried meat, cheese, and hard biscuits. Eating bad food could cause vomiting and **diarrhea**. But passengers had to eat whatever and whenever they could. Those who didn't get enough to eat suffered from **malnutrition**, which caused exhaustion and weakness.

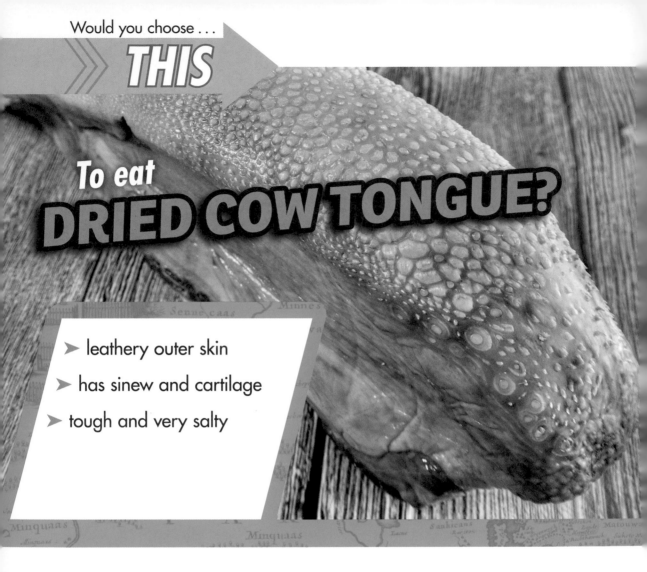

To eat DRIED COW TONGUE?

- ➤ leathery outer skin
- ➤ has sinew and cartilage
- ➤ tough and very salty

People brought foods aboard the *Mayflower* that they hoped would keep on the long journey. Dried cow tongue was one. It was preserved with salt and so was very salty to eat. If not cooked properly, cow tongue is tough. It also has edible **sinew** and **cartilage**. *Mayflower* passengers either ate these chewy features or had to cut them off raw before drying the tongues.

To eat
SALTED FISH?

> fish preserved with dry salt

> chewy

> fishy and salty taste

Passengers also ate salted fish aboard the *Mayflower*. Like cow tongue, this fish was preserved with salt and tasted very salty. There was little fresh water onboard to wash the salt off. In addition to salt, the meat had a fishy flavor. The fish was also very chewy.

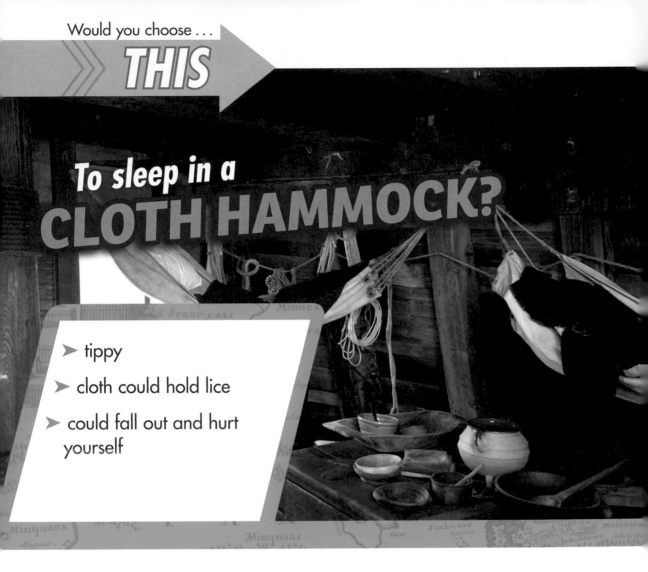

To sleep in a CLOTH HAMMOCK?

➤ tippy
➤ cloth could hold lice
➤ could fall out and hurt yourself

Most passengers slept on the floor below deck. But some hung cloth **hammocks** to sleep in. A hammock would be difficult to get in and out of, especially as the ship swayed. In bad storms, a passenger might also fall out of a hammock. And, just like clothes, a hammock could hold lice.

To sleep in the **SHALLOP?**

➤ small boat stored onboard

➤ hard and cramped

➤ damaged from so many people sleeping in it

The shallop was a small boat that measured about 30 feet (9 m) long. It was stored aboard the *Mayflower*. The shallop carried people to shore upon arrival in America. During the journey, it served as a hard, wooden bed for some passengers. The shallop was cramped. So many people slept in it that the boat's seams separated.

Would you choose . . .

THIS

To be a
CARPENTER?

➤ must make ship repairs, even in severe weather

➤ possibility of injury

➤ ship could sink if you can't fix it

The ship's carpenter plugged leaks and fixed any damage caused by storms. The carpenter had a lot of responsibility. If he couldn't fix the ship, it might sink or have to turn around. During one storm, the *Mayflower*'s main beam cracked. Luckily, the carpenter was able to fix it with a large screw.

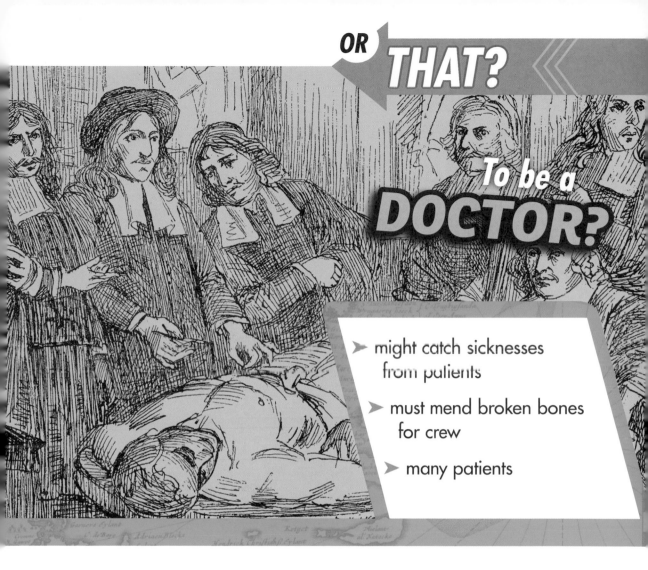

To be a
DOCTOR?

> might catch sicknesses from patients

> must mend broken bones for crew

> many patients

The *Mayflower* doctor saw gross injuries and sick people all day. This included people with **contagious** diseases. Doctors at the time did not know as much about medicine as they do today. Some of their treatments could do more harm than good. Over half the ship's passengers became sick and died after reaching Plymouth Colony. This meant a lot of work for the doctor.

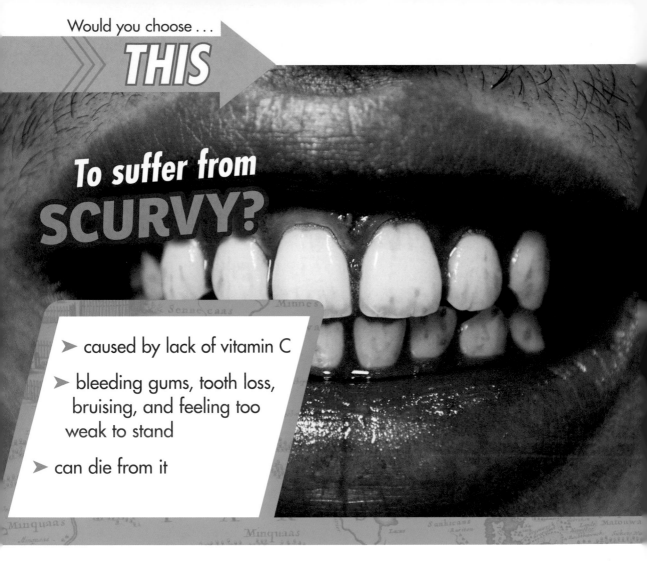

To suffer from SCURVY?

- ➤ caused by lack of vitamin C
- ➤ bleeding gums, tooth loss, bruising, and feeling too weak to stand
- ➤ can die from it

Scurvy is caused by a lack of vitamin C. People get vitamin C by eating fresh fruits and vegetables. *Mayflower* passengers ran out of these foods. Many developed scurvy. The condition causes bleeding gums, bruising, and tooth loss. It also makes people weak. Scurvy doesn't spread to others. But combined with other illnesses, it can be deadly.

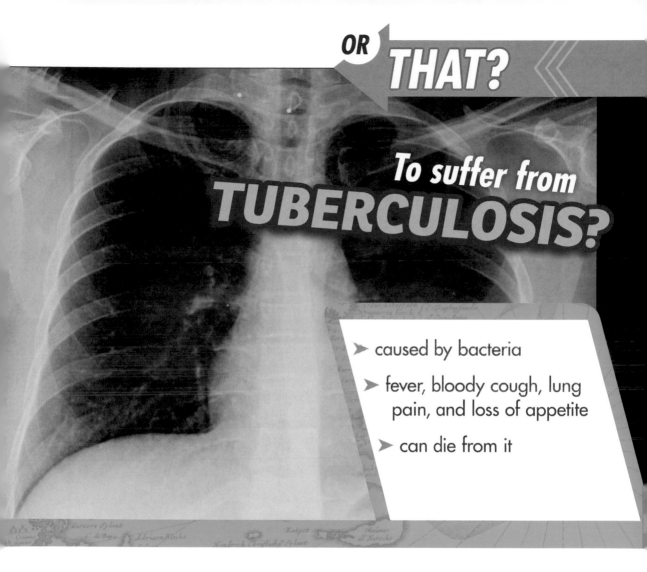

To suffer from
TUBERCULOSIS?

- ➤ caused by bacteria
- ➤ fever, bloody cough, lung pain, and loss of appetite
- ➤ can die from it

Tuberculosis is caused by bacteria. The bacteria spreads when a sick person sneezes or coughs. Tuberculosis spread easily on the cramped ship. The sickness causes fever, a bloody cough, lung pain, and loss of appetite. There was no medicine to treat tuberculosis in the 1600s. Passengers could easily die from it.

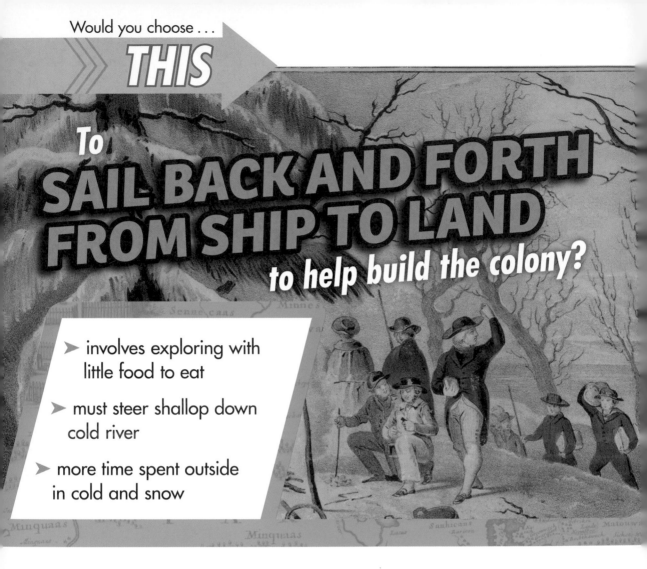

THIS

To
SAIL BACK AND FORTH
FROM SHIP TO LAND
to help build the colony?

➤ involves exploring with little food to eat

➤ must steer shallop down cold river

➤ more time spent outside in cold and snow

Men left the *Mayflower* to explore the land and find a place to settle. This meant steering in cold rivers in the small shallop. And because food supplies were low, it also meant exploring with little food to restore energy. On land, men could build bonfires for warmth. But they were also more exposed to the weather than passengers back on the ship.

To
STAY ONLY ON THE SHIP
during the first winter?

➤ time partially spent caring for sick people

➤ no heaters aboard to keep warm

➤ danger of falling off ship

Some passengers and crew stayed onboard the ship the entire winter upon arrival in America. They spent time caring for sick people. This put these passengers at a greater risk of becoming sick themselves. The passengers would have gotten some heat from the fireboxes used to cook meals. But the ship environment was still cold and damp.

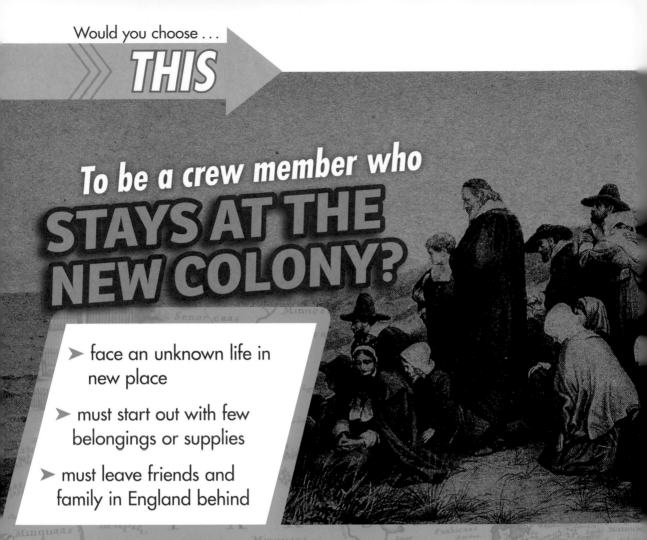

To be a crew member who
STAYS AT THE NEW COLONY?

➤ face an unknown life in new place

➤ must start out with few belongings or supplies

➤ must leave friends and family in England behind

Staying in the New World meant facing an unknown life in a new place. Plymouth Colony was much different from England. Everything from the soil to the weather was new. Those who stayed built new homes and lives starting with few supplies or belongings. Staying also meant leaving behind any friends and family back in England who hadn't come along.

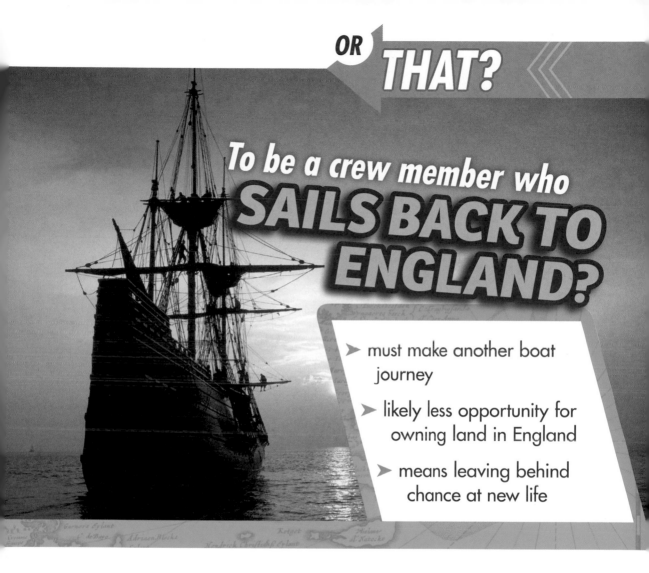

To be a crew member who SAILS BACK TO ENGLAND?

- ➤ must make another boat journey
- ➤ likely less opportunity for owning land in England
- ➤ means leaving behind chance at new life

Crew members who sailed back to England had to make another long journey. Many were weakened by sicknesses they'd fought during winter. Sailing back also meant leaving behind an opportunity to own land. It was hard for a working person to own land in England. But in the new colony, colonists received "family plots" of land.

➤ must dig in dirt

➤ soil held many stones, making it difficult to dig by hand

➤ must fertilize soil with dead fish

The Wampanoags taught the colonists how to grow food in their new home. The most important crop was maize, or corn. Planting maize was hard, dirty work. Colonists dug holes by hand in dry, rocky soil. Then they placed smelly, dead fish in each hole as **fertilizer**.

OR THAT?

To HUNT FOR EELS?

> must hunt in winter, so you would get cold

> involves digging eels out of the mud at the bottoms of ponds

> eels are slimy

The Wampanoag also taught the colonists to hunt eels. Eels were easiest to catch in winter. They **hibernated** in the muddy bottoms of ponds. The colonists had to dig in the mud and spear the eels to catch them. This was cold, dirty work. The eels were also slimy to touch.

LIGHTNING ROUND

Would you choose to . . .

➤ have bugs in your food or rats in your food?

➤ have a pet cat or pet dog on the ship?

➤ eat dried fish or stewed cabbage?

➤ bring along your favorite book or favorite toy?

➤ pass time below deck by reading or playing marbles?

➤ sleep near a water leak or near the slop bucket?

➤ have bedbugs or head lice?

➤ steer the ship or cook meals for the crew?

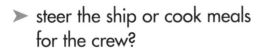

GLOSSARY

cartilage (KAHR-tuh-lij)—a strong, elastic tissue that lines bones at the joints in people and animals

contagious (kuhn-TAY-juhs)—spread by direct or indirect contact with an infected person or animal

diarrhea (dye-uh-REE-uh)—a condition in which normally solid waste from your body becomes liquid

fertilizer (FUR-tuh-lyz-ur)—a substance put into soil to make plants grow better

hammock (HAM-uhk)—a piece of strong net or cloth strung up by two ends and used as a bed

hibernate (HYE-bur-nate)—when animals sleep for the entire winter to help survive low temperatures and scarce food supplies

malnutrition (mal-noo-TRISH-uhn)—sickness or weakness caused by not eating enough food, or by not eating enough healthy food

pitch (PICH)—to plunge or move forward or up and down suddenly

sinew (SIN-yoo)—a band of tissue that connects a muscle to bone

tension (TEN-shuhn)—a feeling of stress, nervousness, or difficulty in a relationship

vomit (VAH-mit)—to bring up food from the stomach and expel it through the mouth

READ MORE

Lusted, Marcia Amidon. *The Mayflower Compact*. North Mankato, MN: Capstone Press, an imprint of Pebble, 2020.

Son, John. *If You Were a Kid on the Mayflower*. New York: Children's Press, an imprint of Scholastic Inc., 2018.

Troupe, Thomas Kingsley. *The Pilgrims' Voyage to America*. North Mankato, MN: Picture Window Books, a Capstone imprint, 2017.

INTERNET SITES

Ducksters—Colonial America: Mayflower
https://www.ducksters.com/history/colonial_america/mayflower.php

Plimoth Plantation—Mayflower and Mayflower Compact
https://www.plimoth.org/learn/just-kids/homework-help
/mayflower-and-mayflower-compact

Scholastic—The First Thanksgiving: Voyage on the Mayflower
https://www.scholastic.com/scholastic_thanksgiving/voyage/